PIANO · VOCAL · GUITAR

43 COUNTRY STANDARDS

4 DECADES OF GREAT COUNTRY SONGS

ISBN 0-7935-6680-0

HAL·LEONARD® CORPORATION

7777 W. BLUEMOUND RD. P.O. BOX 13819 MILWAUKEE, WI 53213

Copyright © 1996 by HAL LEONARD CORPORATION
International Copyright Secured   All Rights Reserved

For all works contained herein:
Unauthorized copying, arranging, adapting, recording or public performance is an infringement of copyright.
Infringers are liable under the law.

43 COUNTRY STANDARDS

CONTENTS

**Achy Breaky Heart
(Don't Tell My Heart)** 4
Billy Ray Cyrus

All the Gold in California 13
The Gatlin Brothers

Always on My Mind 10
Willie Nelson

Angel of the Morning 16
Juice Newton

Ballad of a Teenage Queen 20
Johnny Cash

Boot Scootin' Boogie 22
Brooks & Dunn

Bouquet of Roses 26
Eddy Arnold

Chattahoochee 28
Alan Jackson

Coward of the County 32
Kenny Rogers

Crazy Arms 46
Ray Price

Crying 43
Roy Orbison

Distant Drums 48
Jim Reeves

For the Good Times 51
Ray Price

Friends in Low Places 54
Garth Brooks

The Gambler 60
Kenny Rogers

Hard Rock Bottom of Your Heart 67
Randy Travis

He'll Have to Go 77
Jim Reeves

Hello Walls 74
Faron Young

**Help Me Make It
Through the Night** 80
Sammi Smith

Here You Come Again 86
Dolly Parton

Hey, Good Lookin'................83
Hank Williams

Houston (Means I'm
One Day Closer to You)............90
Larry Gatlin & The Gatlin Brothers

I Believe in You..................100
Don Williams

I Can Love You Like That..........95
John Michael Montgomery

I Love a Rainy Night..............104
Eddie Rabbitt

I'm Movin' On.....................106
Hank Snow

I've Come to Expect It from You...108
George Strait

In Dreams.........................112
Roy Orbison

The Keeper of the Stars...........117
Tracy Byrd

Lookin' for Love..................122
Johnny Lee

Lost in the Fifties Tonight
(In the Still of the Nite)........127
Ronnie Milsap

Love Without End, Amen............130
George Strait

Luckenbach, Texas
(Back to the Basics of Love)......136
Waylon Jennings

No One Else on Earth..............140
Wynonna Judd

Oh, Pretty Woman..................144
Roy Orbison

Please Help Me, I'm Falling
(In Love with You)................154
Hank Locklin

Ring of Fire......................151
Johnny Cash

Snowbird..........................156
Anne Murray

When You Say Nothing at All.......159
Keith Whitley

When You're Hot, You're Hot.......164
Jerry Reed

Why Not Me........................167
The Judds

Wings of a Dove...................173
Ferlin Husky

Wolverton Mountain................170
Claude King

ACHY BREAKY HEART
(DON'T TELL MY HEART)

Words and Music by
DON VON TRESS

ALWAYS ON MY MIND

Words and Music by WAYNE THOMPSON, MARK JAMES and JOHNNY CHRISTOPHER

© 1971, 1979 SCREEN GEMS-EMI MUSIC INC. and BUDDE SONGS INC.
All Rights Controlled and Administered by SCREEN GEMS-EMI MUSIC INC.
All Rights Reserved International Copyright Secured Used by Permission

All The Gold In California

Words and Music by
LARRY GATLIN

Additional Lyrics

4. Very soon she was a star, pretty house and shiny cars,
   Swimming pool and a fence around, but she missed her old home town.
   (But she missed her old home town)
   All the world was at her door,
   All except the boy next door, who worked at the candy store.
   Dream on, dream on, teenage queen, saddest girl we've ever seen.

5. Then one day the teenage star sold her house and all her cars.
   Gave up all her wealth and fame, left it all and caught a train.
   (Left it all and caught a train)
   Do I have to tell you more?
   She came back to the boy next door, who worked at the candy store.
   Now this story has some more; you'll hear it all at the candy store.

BOUQUET OF ROSES

Words and Music by STEVE NELSON and BOB HILLIARD

CHATTAHOOCHEE

*Words and Music by JIM McBRIDE
and ALAN JACKSON*

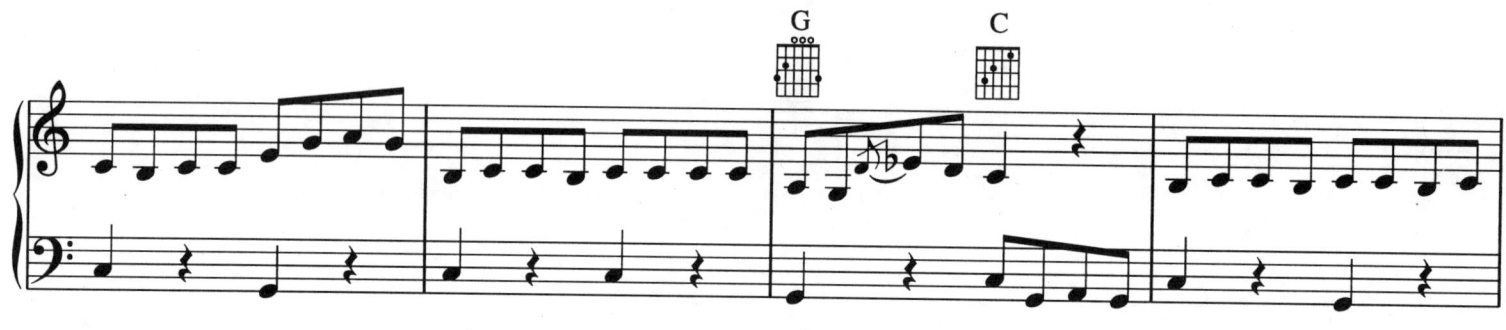

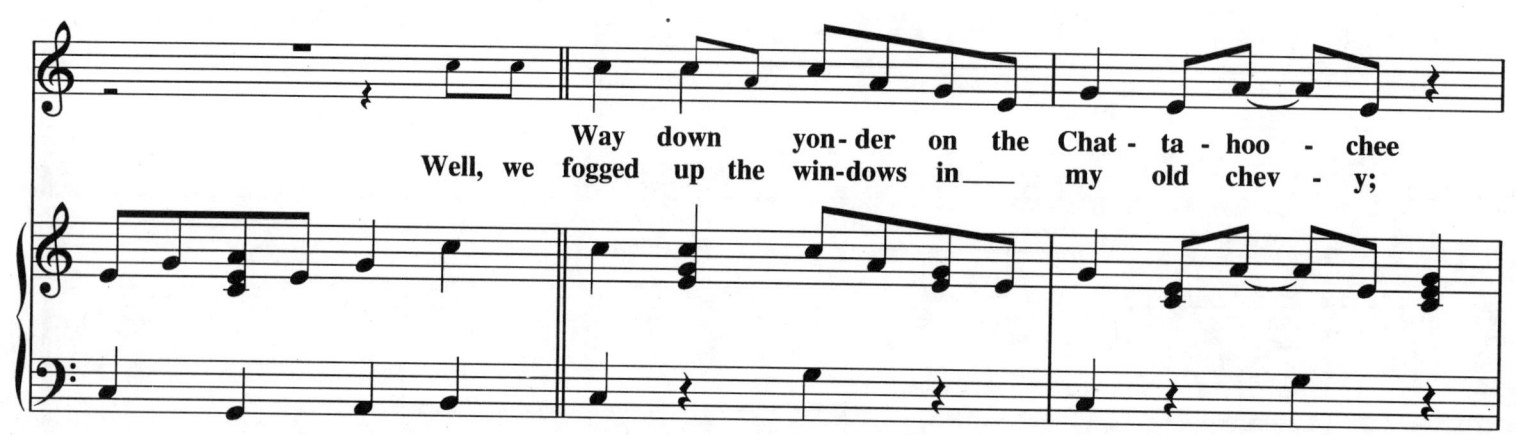

Way down yon-der on the Chat-ta-hoo-chee
Well, we fogged up the win-dows in___ my old chev-y;

Copyright © 1992 Sony/ATV Tunes LLC, Seventh Son Music and Mattie Ruth Musick
All Rights on behalf of Sony/ATV Tunes LLC Administered by Sony/ATV Music Publishing, 8 Music Square West, Nashville, TN 37203
International Copyright Secured All Rights Reserved

(Spoken) there was three of them! *(Sung)* Tommy opened up the door and saw his Becky cryin', The torn dress, the shattered look was more than he could stand. He reached above the fireplace and took down his daddy's picture.

As his tears fell on his dad-dy's face, he heard these words a-gain: "Prom-ise me son, not to do the things I've done, Walk a-way from trou-ble if you can. It won't mean you're weak if you turn the oth-er cheek,__ I hope you're old e-nough to un-der-stand:__ Son, you don't have to fight__ to be a man".__ The Gat-lin boys_ just laughed_ at him_ when he walked in-to the bar-room. One of them_ got up__ and met him half-

40

-way 'cross the floor.___ When Tommy turned_ a-round___ they said, "Hey look! ol' yel-low's leav-in'." *(Spoken)* But you coulda heard a pin drop when Tommy stopped and blocked the door. *(Sung)* Twen-ty years of crawl-in'___ was bot-tled up___ in-side him, He was-n't hold-in' noth-in' back___ he let 'em have it all.___ When Tommy left__ the bar-room not a Gatlin boy was standin', He said, "This one's__ for Becky." As he watched the last one fall. *(Spoken) And I heard him say,* "I promised you, Dad,___ not to do___ the things you done, I walk away from trouble when I can.___

42

Now please don't think I'm weak, I didn't turn the other cheek, And Poppa, I sure hope you understand: Sometimes you gotta fight when you're a man." Ev-'ry-one considered him the coward of the county.

Slower

Guitar Tacet

CRYING

Words and Music by ROY ORBISON
and JOE MELSON

Moderately slow, with feeling

I was all right for a while; I could smile for a while, but I saw you last night; you held my hand real tight, as you stopped to say, "Hel-lo." Oh, you

I was o-ver you so true, so true, I love you e-ven more than I did be-fore, but dar-ling, what can I do? For you

Copyright © 1961 (Renewed 1989) BARBARA ORBISON MUSIC COMPANY, ORBI-LEE MUSIC, R-KEY DARKUS MUSIC and ACUFF-ROSE MUSIC, INC.
International Copyright Secured   All Rights Reserved

wished me well; you couldn't tell that I'd been
don't love me and I'll al - ways be

cry - ing o - ver you, cry - ing
cry - ing o - ver you, cry - ing

o - ver you. When you said, "So
o - ver you. Yes, now you're

long"; left me stand - ing all a - lone, a - lone and
gone and from this mo - ment on I'll be

C
C+
F/C
cry - ing, cry - ing, cry - ing,
cry - ing, cry - ing, cry - ing,
Fm/C
C
cry - ing. It's hard to un - der - stand, but the
cry - ing. Yeah, cry - ing,
G7
1 C
touch of your hand can start me cry - ing.
cry - ing o - ver
2 C
I thought that you.

CRAZY ARMS

Words and Music by RALPH MOONEY
and CHARLES SEALS

Moderately

Blue is not the word for the way that I feel. And a
Please take the trea-sured dreams I've had for you and me; And

storm is brew-ing in this heart of mine. This is no
take all the love I thought was mine. Some-day my

trea-sured dream, I know that it's real. You're some-one else-'s love now; you're not
cra-zy arms will hold some-one new. But now I'm so lone-ly all the

Copyright © 1955, 1956 Sony/ATV Songs LLC and Champion Music Corporation
Copyright Renewed
All Rights on behalf of Sony/ATV Songs LLC Administered by Sony/ATV Music Publishing, 8 Music Square West, Nashville, TN 37203
Champion Music Corporation is an MCA company
International Copyright Secured   All Rights Reserved

47

DISTANT DRUMS

Words and Music by
CINDY WALKER

call, for me to come, then I must go,
call, then I must go, across the sea, so wild and

then I must go, and you must
a - cross the sea, so wild and

stay. So, Mary, marry me,
grey. So, Mary, marry me,

let's not wait. Let's share
let's not wait. Or the

all the time we can be-fore it's too late.
dis - tant drums might change our wed-ding day.

Love me now, for now is all the time there may be.

If you love me, Mary, Ma - ry, Ma - ry, mar - ry me.

I hear the me.

FOR THE GOOD TIMES

Words and Music by
KRIS KRISTOFFERSON

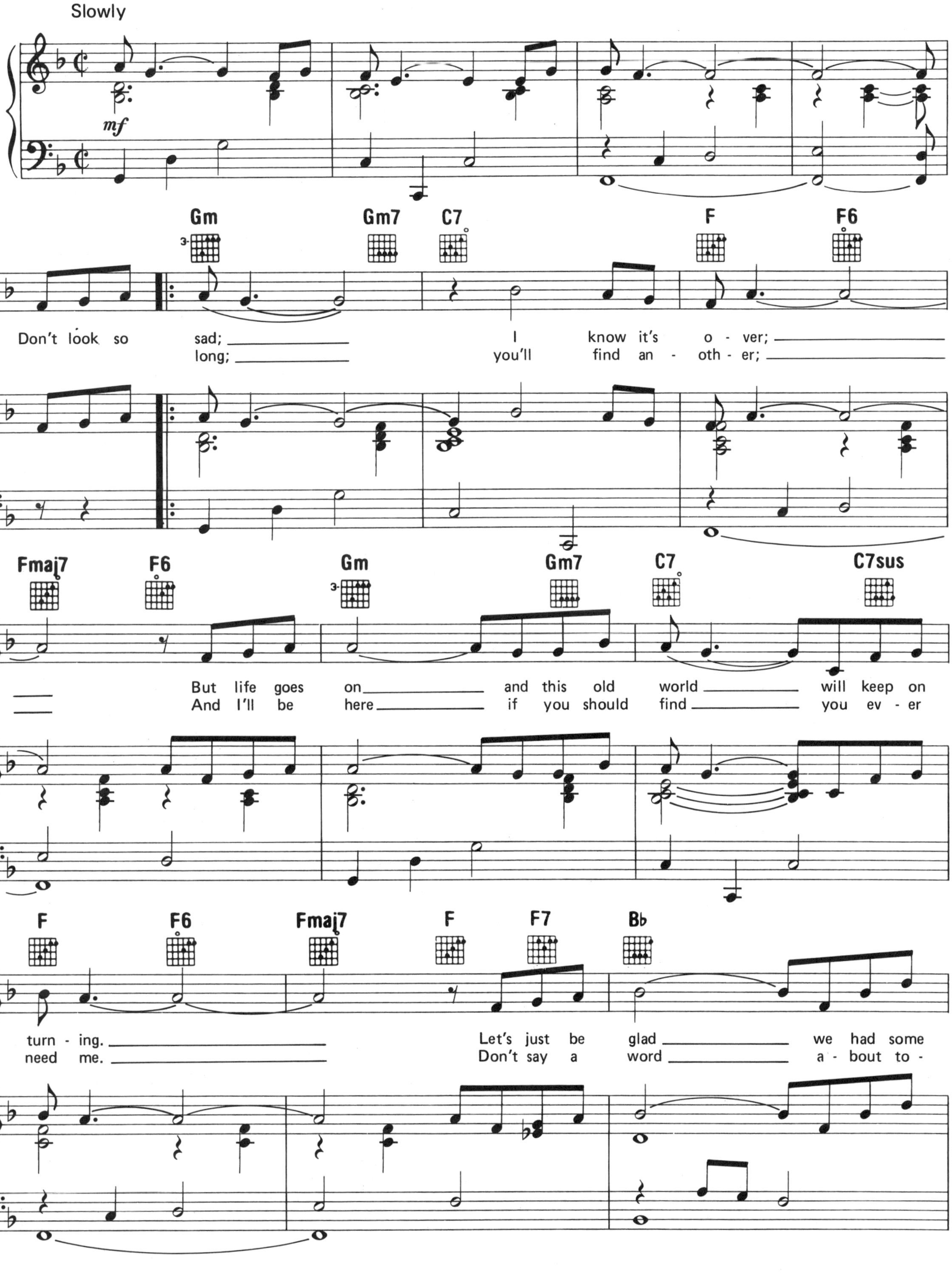

time____ to spend to-geth-er.____ There's no
mor-row____ or for-ev-er.____ There'll be

need to watch the bridg-es that we're burn-ing.____
time e-nough for sad-ness when you leave me.____

Guitar Tacet

____ Lay your head____ up-on my

pil-low,____ Hold your warm____ and ten-der

body - y close to mine. _____ Hear the whis - per of the rain - drops blow - ing soft a - gainst the win - dow And make be - lieve you love me _____ one more time _____ For the good times. _____ I'll get a - good times. _____

FRIENDS IN LOW PLACES

Words and Music by DEWAYNE BLACKWELL
and EARL BUD LEE

last one to show;__ I was the last__ one you thought you'd see there.__ And I saw the sur-prise__ and the fear in his eyes__ when I took his glass__ of cham-pagne__ and I toast-ed you,__ said, "Hon-ey,

just say good-night__ and I'll show__ my-self__ to the door.__ Hey, I did-n't mean__ to cause a big scene__ just give me an ho-ur and then,__ well I'll be as high__ as that i-

we may be through__ but you'll nev-er hear__ me com-plain."__
-vo - ry tow - er that you're liv - in' in.__

'Cause I've got friends__ in low plac - es where the whis-key__ drowns__ and the beer__ chas - es my blues__ a - way and I'll be o - kay.__

Yeah, I'm not big on so-cial grac-es. Think I'll slip on down to the o-a-sis. Oh, I've got friends in low plac-es.

D.S. al Coda

Well, I

CODA

I've got friends in low places where the whis-key drowns and the beer chas-es my blues a - way and I'll be o - kay.

Yeah, I'm not big on so - cial grac - es. Think I'll slip on down to the o - a - sis. Oh, I've got friends in low plac - es.

Repeat and Fade

THE GAMBLER

Words and Music by
DON SCHLITZ

Moderate country

On a warm summers eve-nin' On a train bound for no-
son I've made a life out of read-in' peo-ples fac-

-where I met up with the gam-bler We were
-es And know-in' what their cards were by the

both too tired to sleep, So we took turns a star-
way they held their eyes. And if you don't mind my say-

*Copyright © 1977 Sony/ATV Tunes LLC
All Rights Administered by Sony/ATV Music Publishing, 8 Music Square West, Nashville, TN 37203
International Copyright Secured All Rights Reserved*

-in' out the win-dow at the dark-ness 'til
-in' I can see you're out of a-ces For a

bore-dom o-ver-took us And he be-gan to speak He said,

taste of your whis-key I'll give you some ad-vice

So I hand-ed him my bot-tle and he drank down my last

swal - low. Then he bummed a cig - a - rette and asked me for a light.

And the night got death - ly qui - et, and his face lost all ex - pres - sion said "If you're gon - na play the game, boy ya got - ta learn to play it right.

You got to know how to hold 'em, know when to fold

'em, know when to walk a-way and know when to run. You nev-er count your mon-ey when you're sit-tin' at the ta--ble there'll be time e-nough for count-in' when the deal-in's done

Ev'-ry gam-bler knows that the se-cret to sur-viv-in is know-in what to throw a-way and know-in what to keep. 'cause ev-'ry hands a win-ner and ev-'ry hands a los-er and the best that you can hope for is to die in your sleep. And when he'd finished speakin', he turned back towards the window crushed out his cigarette and faded off to sleep. And somewhere in the darkness the gambler he broke even but in his final words I found an ace that I could keep. You got to

A
E
know when to hold ___ 'em, know when to fold ___ 'em,
A
E
B
know when to walk ___ a - way_ and know when to run. ___ You nev - er
E
B9
E
A
E
count your mon-ey when you're sit - tin' at the ta - ble there'll be
A
E
B
1,2
E
3
E
time e - nough_ for count - in' when the deal - in's done "You got to done."

HARD ROCK BOTTOM OF YOUR HEART

Words and Music by
HUGH PRESTWOOD

Moderately fast Country

Since the day ___ I was led ___ to ___ temp-
___ that we built ___ is ___ still ___

ta- tion, ___ and in weak- ness ___ did
stand- ing. ___ Its foun- da- tion ___ is

Copyright © 1989 by Careers-BMG Music Publishing, Inc. and Hugh Prestwood Music
All Rights Administered by Careers-BMG Music Publishing, Inc.
International Copyright Secured   All Rights Reserved

68

me. And you keep say-ing you can't e-ven start. And I feel like a stone you have picked up and thrown to the hard rock bot-

B
E
- tom of your heart, to the hard
A
B
E
To Coda
1
rock bot - tom of your heart. Now this home
2
Bm
A
Bm
We can't just block it out. We've got to
A
Bm
A
talk it out un - til our hearts get back in

touch._____ I need your love, I miss it. I can't go __ on like this, it hurts too much. _____

Instrumental solo

Solo ends **And I keep**

CODA

To the hard rock bot-tom of your heart,

to the hard rock bot-

-tom of your heart.

Whoo,_____ whoo,_____

whoo._____

Repeat and Fade

HELLO WALLS

Words and Music by
WILLIE NELSON

1. Hel-lo, walls, how'd things go for you to-day? Don't you miss her since she up and walked a-way? And I'll bet you dread to spend an-oth-er

   win-dow, well, I see that you're still here. Aren't you lone-ly since our dar-lin' dis-ap-peared? Well, look here, is that a tear-drop in the

Copyright © 1961 Sony/ATV Songs LLC
Copyright Renewed
All Rights Administered by Sony/ATV Music Publishing, 8 Music Square West, Nashville, TN 37203
International Copyright Secured   All Rights Reserved

75

C C7 F C
Guitar Tacet
ceil - ing, I'm gon - na stare at you a - while you know I
C D7 G7
can't sleep, so won't you bear with me a - while? We must
3
F C
all pull to - geth - er or else I'll lose my mind, 'cause I've got a
mf
F C G7 C
feel - in' she'll be gone a long, long time.

HE'LL HAVE TO GO

Words and Music by JOE ALLISON
and AUDREY ALLISON

Moderato

Put your sweet lips a lit-tle clo-ser to the phone ___ Let's pre-tend that we're to-geth-er all a-lone ___ I'll tell the man to turn the juke-box way down low ___ And you can tell your friend there with you he'll have to go ___

© 1959 (Renewed 1987) BEECHWOOD MUSIC CORP.
All Rights Reserved   International Copyright Secured   Used by Permission

78

Whis-per to me tell me do you love me true____ Or is he hold-ing you the way I do?____ Tho' love is blind make up your mind I've got to know____ Should I hang up or will you tell him he'll have to go ____ You can't say the words I want to hear while you're with an-oth-er man If you want me an-swer

F C7 F B♭
"Yes" or "No" dar-ling I will un-der-stand Put your sweet lips a lit-tle clo-ser to the
F Gm7
phone Let's pre-tend that we're to-geth-er all a-lone
C7 F F7 B♭
I'll tell the man to turn the juke-box way down low And you can
F C7
tell your friend there with you he'll have to
1 F B♭ F C7
go Put your
2 F B♭ F
go

HELP ME MAKE IT THROUGH THE NIGHT

Words and Music by
KRIS KRISTOFFERSON

Moderato

Take the rib-bon from your hair,
Come and lay down by my side
Yes-ter-day is dead and gone

Shake it loose and let it
Till the ear-ly morn-in'
And to-mor-row's out of

fall,
light.
sight,

Lay-in' soft up-on my
All I'm tak-in' is your
And it's sad to be a-

© 1970 TEMI COMBINE INC.
All Rights Controlled by COMBINE MUSIC CORP. and Administered by EMI BLACKWOOD MUSIC INC.
All Rights Reserved International Copyright Secured Used by Permission

A7
To Coda
1
skin.
time.
lone.
Like the shad - ows on the
D
G
wall.
2
Help me make it thru the
D
G
night.
D
I don't care who's right or
G
wrong,
I don't try to un - der -

stand._____ Let the dev-il take to-

mor-row._____ Lord, to-night I need a

friend._____ Help me make it thru the night._____

HEY, GOOD LOOKIN'

Words and Music by
HANK WILLIAMS

Moderately

Hey, Hey, Good Look-in' What-cha got cook-in' How's a-bout cook-in' some-thin' up with me
Hey, free and read-y So we can go stead-y How's a-bout sav-in' all your time for me

Hey, sweet
No more

Copyright © 1951 by Hiriam Music and Acuff-Rose Music, Inc. in the U.S.A.
Copyright Renewed
All Rights for Hiriam Music Administered by Rightsong Music, Inc.
All Rights outside the U.S.A. Controlled by Acuff-Rose Music, Inc.
International Copyright Secured   All Rights Reserved

ba - by,
look - in', I   Don't____ you think   may - be
              know____ I've been   took - en

D7 We could find us a brand new rec - i - pe____
G7 How's a-bout keep-in' stead - y com - pa - ny____
C

C7 I got a hot rod Ford and a two dol - lar bill and
F I'm gon - na throw my date book____ o - ver the fence and
C

F I know a spot right o - ver the hill____
find me____ one right for five or ten cents____
C There's so - da pop and the
I'll keep it 'til it's____
F

dan - cin's free, so if you wan - na have fun come a - long with me
cov - ered with age 'Cause I'm writ - in' your name down on ev - 'ry page

Hey, Good Look - in' What - cha got cook - in'
Hey, Good Look - in' What - cha got cook - in'

How's a - bout cook - in' some - thin' up with me.
How's a - bout cook - in' some - thin' up with

I'm me.

HERE YOU COME AGAIN

Words by CYNTHIA WEIL
Music by BARRY MANN

Moderate
♩ = 106

Here you come a-gain, just when I've be-gun to get my-
Here you come a-gain, just when I'm a-bout to make it

self to-geth-er, you waltz right in the door, just like you've done be-fore and
work with-out you, you look in-to my eyes and lie those pret-ty lies and

1. wrap my heart 'round your lit-tle fin-ger.
2. pret-ty soon I'm wond-'rin how I

© 1977 SCREEN GEMS-EMI MUSIC INC. and SUMMERHILL SONGS INC.
All Rights Controlled and Administered by SCREEN GEMS-EMI MUSIC INC.
All Rights Reserved   International Copyright Secured   Used by Permission

came to doubt you. All you got-ta do is smile that smile and there go all my de-fens-es. Just leave it up to you and in a lit-tle while you're mess-in' up my mind and fill-in' up my sens-es.

Here you come a-gain look-in' bet-ter than a bod-y

(2nd time instrumental

has a right __ to; __ and shak-in' me __ up so that all I real-ly know is here you come a-gain __ and here I __ go. __ All you got-ta do __ is smile that smile __ and there go all __ my __ de-fens-es. __ Just leave it up __ to you __ and in a lit-tle while __ you're messin' up my mind and fillin' up my senses. Here you come again, lookin' better than a body has a right to and shakin' me up so that all I really know is here you come again and here I go here I go

HOUSTON
(MEANS I'M ONE DAY CLOSER TO YOU)

Words and Music by
LARRY GATLIN

Moderately fast Western Swing

Hous - ton,___ Hous - ton means that I'm one day clos - er to you.___

© 1983 TEMI COMBINE INC. and SONGS OF ALL NATIONS
All Rights for TEMI COMBINE INC. Controlled by COMBINE MUSIC CORP. and Administered by EMI Blackwood Music Inc.
All Rights Reserved   International Copyright Secured   Used by Permission

Oh honey, Houston,

Houston means the last day of the tour and we're through.

Well honey, you and

God in heaven above knows I love what I do

for a livin'; I do. Oh, but Houston, Houston means that I'm one day closer to you. Yeah, singin' at the world's biggest rodeo show was a great time for me and the guys. Ah, but when I'm a-way from you, hon-ey, time al-ways nev-er flies. And sleep-in' all a-lone in that Hol-i-day ho-tel sure makes a cow-boy blue. But here I am in Hous-ton and I'm one day clos-er to you.

D.S. al Coda

Coda

Yeah hon-ey, Hous-ton, Hous-ton means that I'm one day clos-er to you.

I CAN LOVE YOU LIKE THAT

Words and Music by STEVE DIAMOND,
MARIBETH DERRY and JENNIFER KIMBALL

Moderate Ballad

With pedal

They read you Cin-der-el-la, you hoped it would come true that one day your Prince Charm-ing would come rescue you. You

nev-er make a prom-ise I don't in-tend to keep. So, when I say for-ev-er, for-ev-er's what I mean.

© 1995 Diamond Cuts, Criterion Music Corp., Full Keel Music Co., Second Wave Music and Friends And Angels Music
All Rights for Diamond Cuts in the U.S. and Canada Administered by Seven Summits Music
All Rights for Second Wave Music and Friends And Angels Music Administered by Full Keel Music Co.
International Copyright Secured   All Rights Reserved

like ro-man-tic mov-ies; you nev-er will for-get the way you felt when Ro-me-o kissed Ju-li-et. All this time that you've been wait-ing, you don't have to wait no more.

I'm no Ca-sa-no-va, but I swear this much is true: I'll be hold-ing noth-ing back when it comes to you. You dream of love that's ev-er-last-ing. Well, ba-by, o-pen up your eyes.

I can love you like that. I would make you my world, move heav-en and earth

97

You want ten-der-ness, I got ten-der-ness. And I see through to the heart of you. If you want a man who un-der-stands, you don't have to look ver-y far.

[G] I can love you, I ___ can, I can love you like that. [C] I would make you my world, ___ [Em] move heaven and earth ___ [F] if you were my girl. ___ [G7sus] I will give you my heart, [C] be all that you need, ___ [Em] show you you're ev-[F]'ry-thing that's precious to me. ___ I can love you like that. [G7sus]

Repeat and Fade

I BELIEVE IN YOU

Words and Music by ROGER COOK
and SAM HOGIN

Moderately slow, triplet feel

I don't believe in su-per-stars,— or-gan-ic food— and for-eign cars,— I
don't be-lieve that Heav-en waits,— for on-ly those— who con-gre-gate,— I

don't be-lieve the price of gold,— the cer-tain-ty— of grow-ing old,— that
like to think of God as love,— He's down be-low,— He's up a-bove,— He's

© 1980 SCREEN GEMS-EMI MUSIC INC.
All Rights Reserved International Copyright Secured Used by Permission

right is right and left is wrong, that north and south can't get along, that
watching people ev-'ry-where, He knows who does and does-n't care, and

east is east and west is west and being first is always best; but I believe in love;
I'm an or-di-na-ry man, sometimes I wonder who I am; but I believe in love;

I be-lieve in ba-bies; I be-lieve in Mom and Dad
I be-lieve in mu-sic; I be-lieve in mag-ic

and I be-lieve in you. Well, I
and I be-lieve in you.

I know with all my cer-tain-ty___ what's go-in' on with you and me___ is a good thing, it's true; I be-lieve in you. I don't be-lieve vir-gin-i-ty___ is as com-mon as___ it used to be,___ in work-in' days and sleep-in' nights,___ that black is black___ and white is white, that Su-per-man and Rob-in Hood___ are

still alive in Hollywood, that gasoline's in short supply, the rising cost of gettin' by; but I believe in love; I believe in old folks;
lieve in love; I believe in babies;
Instrumental

I believe in children; I believe in you.
I believe in Mom and Dad

I be- and I believe in you.

D.S. and Fade

I LOVE A RAINY NIGHT

Words and Music by EDDIE RABBITT,
EVEN STEVENS and DAVID MALLOY

Moderately Bright

1.3. Well, I love a rain-y night; I love a rain-y night. I
2.4. a rain-y night; it's such a beau-ti-ful sight. I love to
5. *(Instr. solo ad lib.)*

love to hear the thun-der; watch the light-ning when it lights up the sky.
feel the rain on my face; taste the rain on my lips,

You know it makes me feel good.
in the moon-light shad-ows.

2. Well, I love

(end solo)

© 1980 SCREEN GEMS-EMI MUSIC INC.
All Rights Reserved   International Copyright Secured   Used by Permission

1.,3. Show-ers wash all my cares a-way; I wake up to a sun-ny day, 'cause I love a rain-y night. Yeah, I love a rain-y night. Well, I love a rain-y night. Well, I love a rain-y night, ooh, ooh. I love a rain-y night. Well, I love

2. Puts a song in this heart of mine; puts a smile on my face ev-'ry time,

D.S. after repeat

D.S. al Fine after repeat

I'M MOVIN' ON

Words and Music by
HANK SNOW

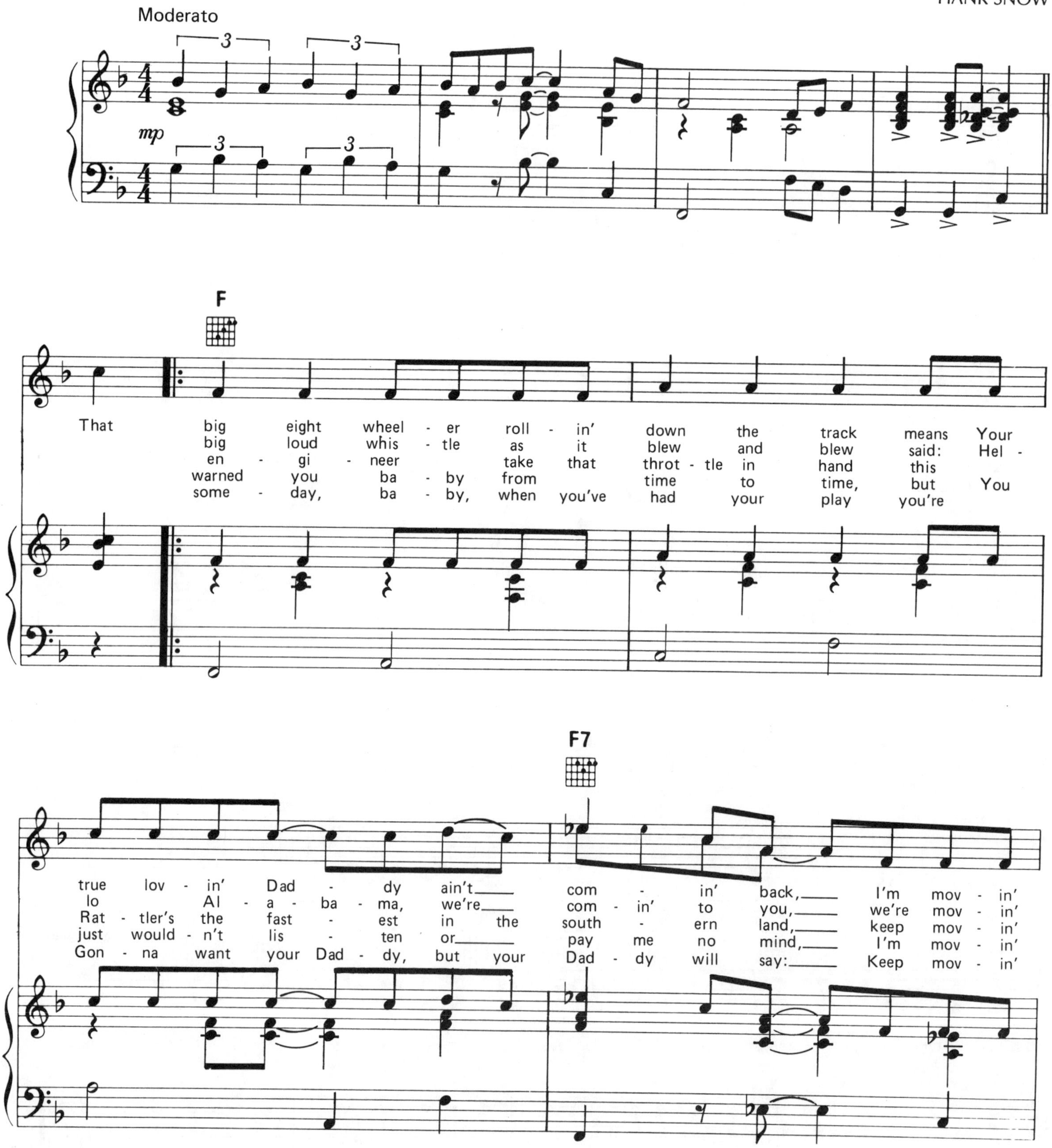

on, I'll soon be gone,
on, Oh, hear my song.
on, Keep roll - in' on.
on, I'm roll - in' on.
on, You stayed a-way too long.

You were fly - in' too high for my lit - tle old sky, so I'm mov - in'
You had the laugh on me, so I've set you free and I'm mov - in'
You're gon - na ease my mind, so put me there on time, keep roll - in'
You have bro - ken your vow and it's all o - ver now, so I'm mov - in'
I'm through with you, too bad you are blue, so keep mov - in'

on.
on.
on. That
on. Mis - ter
on. I
But

I'VE COME TO EXPECT IT FROM YOU

Words and Music by DEAN DILLON
and BUDDY CANNON

Moderate Two-Beat

1. So up-set,
2. A mil-lion times,
3. *Instrumental*
4. I could raise hell,

A nerv-ous wreck. can't be-lieve you said good-bye.
A mil-lion lines and I bought 'em ev-'ry-one.
But what the hell, it would-n't do a bit of good.

© Copyright 1990 by MUSIC CORPORATION OF AMERICA, INC., JESSIE JO MUSIC, BUDDY CANNON MUSIC and POLYGRAM INTERNATIONAL PUBLISHING, INC.
All Rights for JESSIE JO MUSIC Controlled and Administered by MUSIC CORPORATION OF AMERICA, INC.
International Copyright Secured   All Rights Reserved
MCA music publishing

Sit and smoke, ... cry and joke
You don't care. .... You rip
Pack and leave, ... my heart a-

tear .... a - bout .... these tears in .... my eyes.
.... ev - 'ry dream I've count - ed on.
grees it seems to think that .... I should.

1., 3. How could you do .... what you've
2. I guess that I .... should thank .... my
4. There won't be .... no more

G#+
C/G
gone and done to me?
I would-n't
un - luck - y stars
that I'm a - live
next time do - in' me wrong.
You'll come
D
treat a dog the way you treat - ed me.
and you're the way you are.
back this time to find out that I'm gone.
G7
But that's what I get.
But that's what I get.
But that's what I get.
C
I've come to ex - pect it from you.
I've come to ex - pect it from you.
you should ex - pect that from me.

111

That's what I get. I've come to ex - pect it from you.

IN DREAMS

Words and Music by
ROY ORBISON

Moderately

A can-dy col-ored clown they call the sand-man tip-toes to my room ev-'ry night just to sprin-kle star-dust and to whis-per, "Go to sleep, ev-'ry-thing is al-right." I close my eyes, then I drift a-way

Copyright © 1963 (Renewed 1991) BARBARA ORBISON MUSIC COMPANY, ORBI-LEE MUSIC, R-KEY DARKUS MUSIC and ACUFF-ROSE MUSIC, INC.
International Copyright Secured   All Rights Reserved

113

into the magic night. I softly say a silent prayer like dreamers do, then I fall asleep to dream my dreams of you. In dreams I walk with you.

F
G7
C
in dreams I talk to you,
in dreams you're mine.
D7
All the
C
Dm7
G7
C
Dm
time, with you ev - er in dreams, in
G7
C
Fm
dreams.
But just be - fore the

[C] dawn ___ I awake and find you [Fm] gone. ___ I can't help it, I can't help it if I [Dm] cry. ___ I remember that you said, "Good-[G7]... [C] bye." ___ It's too bad that all these [F]

G7
C
F
things can on - ly hap - pen in my
G7
C
dreams, on - ly in
D7
Dm7
G7
dreams, beau - ti - ful
1 C
2 C
dreams. I close my dreams.

THE KEEPER OF THE STARS

Words and Music by DICKEY LEE, DANNY MAYO and KAREN STALEY

Moderately slow

It was no ac-ci-dent, me find-ing you.
Soft moon-light on your face, oh, how you shine.
Some-one had a hand in it
It takes my breath a-way

Copyright © 1994 Songs Of PolyGram International, Inc., Pal Time Music, Sixteen Stars Music, New Haven Music, Inc. and Murrah Music Corp.
International Copyright Secured   All Rights Reserved

long be-fore _ we ev-er knew. Now I ____ just
just to look _ in-to your eyes. I know _ I

can't __ be-lieve __ you're in __ my
don't __ de-serve __ a treas-ure _ like

life. Heav-en's smil-in'
you. There real - ly __

down on me ____ as I look at you _ to -
are no words ___ to show my grat - i -

night.
tude. So, I tip my hat to the Keeper of the Stars. He sure knew what he was doin' when he joined these two hearts. I hold ev - 'ry-

thing when I hold you in my arms. I've got all I'll ever need, thanks to the Keeper of the Stars. Stars.

It was no ac-ci-dent, me find-ing you. Some-one had a hand in it long be-fore we ev-er knew.

LOOKIN' FOR LOVE
from URBAN COWBOY

Words and Music by WANDA MALLETTE,
PATTI RYAN and BOB MORRISON

Moderately

Well, I've spent a life-time look-in' for you;
And I was a-lone ___ then, no love in sight;

sin-gles bars and good time lov-ers were
and I did ev-'ry-thing I could to get me

nev-er true. ___ Play-in' a fool's ___
through the night. ___ Don't know ___ where it start-

© 1980 TEMI COMBINE INC. and SOUTHERN DAYS MUSIC
All Rights for TEMI COMBINE INC. Controlled by MUSIC CITY MUSIC INC. and Administered by EMI APRIL MUSIC INC.
All Rights Reserved   International Copyright Secured   Used by Permission

D
game, hop - in' to win;
- ed or where it might end;
G
D
A
A/G
and tell - in' those sweet lies and los - in' a - gain.
I turned to a stran - ger just like a friend.
A/F#
A/E
D
I was look - in' for love in all the wrong plac - es,
I was look - in' for love in all the wrong plac - es,
look - in' for love in all the wrong plac - es,
F#m
G
look - in' for love in too man - y fac - es, search-in' their eyes and
look - in' for love in too man - y fac - es, search-in' their eyes and
look - in' for love in too man - y fac - es, search-in' their eyes and

lookin' for traces of what I'm dreamin' of.
lookin' for traces of what I'm dreamin' of.
lookin' for traces of what I'm dreamin' of.

Hopin' to find a friend and a lover; I'll bless the day
Hopin' to find a friend and a lover; I'll bless the day
Now that I've found a friend and a lover; I bless the day

I discover another heart lookin' for love.
I discover another heart lookin' for love.
I discovered

Then you came a-knock-in' at my heart's door; you're ev-'ry-thing I've been look-in' for.

No more you, oh you, look-in' for love in all the wrong plac-es;

F♯m
G
in too ___ man - y fac - es, search - in' their eyes ___ and
Em
F♯m
G
A
look - in' for trac - es of what I'm dream - in' of. ___
D
F♯m
Now that I've found ___ a friend ___ and a lov - er; I bless the day ___
G
Em
A
Repeat and Fade
___ I dis - cov - ered you, oh you; look - in' for love ___

LOST IN THE FIFTIES TONIGHT
(IN THE STILL OF THE NITE)

Words and Music by MIKE REID,
TROY SEALS and FRED PARRIS

1. Close your eyes baby, follow my heart, call on the mem-'ries here in the dark. We'll let the magic take us a-way, back to the feeling we

2. See additional lyrics

Copyright © 1984 by BMG Songs, Inc., WB Music Corp., Two Sons Music and Llee Corp.
International Copyright Secured   All Rights Reserved

shared when they'd play: In the still of the night, hold me darling hold me tight. Oh, shoo-doop, shoo-be doo, shoo-doop, doo; so real, so right, lost in the Fif-ties to-night.

Additional Lyrics

These precious hours, we know can't survive.
Love's all that matters while the past is alive.
Now and for always, till time disappears,
We'll hold each other whenever we hear:

LOVE WITHOUT END, AMEN

Words and Music by
AARON G. BARKER

Moderately, with a beat

I got sent home from school one day with a shiner on my eye.
I became a father in the spring of eighty-one.
Fightin' was against the rules and it didn't matter why.
There was no doubt that stubborn boy was just like my Father's son.
When Dad got home I told that story
And when I thought my patience had been

Copyright © 1990 O-Tex Music (BMI) and Bill Butler Music (BMI), 1000 18th Avenue South, Nashville, TN 37212
International Copyright Secured   All Rights Reserved

just like I'd re-hearsed, and then I
test-ed to the end, I

stood there on those trem-blin' knees and wait-ed for the worst.
took my Dad-dy's se-cret and I passed it on to him.

And he said,
I said, "Let me tell you a se-cret a-bout a fa-ther's love, a se-cret that my Dad-dy said was

just be - tween us." (He said,) / (I said,)

"Dad-dy's don't just love their chil-dren ev-'ry now and then, it's a love with-out end, A - men."

It's a love with-out end, A - men.

When ... Last night I dreamed I died and stood outside those pearly gates. When suddenly, I realized there must be some mistake. If they know half the things I've done they'll

nev-er let__ me in._____ And then some-where from the oth-er side I heard these words a-gain.__ And they said, "Let me tell_ you a se-cret_ a-bout_ a fa-ther's_ love, a se-cret that_ my__ dad-dy said__ was

just be-tween___ us." You see,

dad-dy's just_ don't love_ their chil-dren ev-'ry now_ and then,_____

it's a love with-out end,__ A - men. It's a

love with-out end,__ A - men.

LUCKENBACH, TEXAS
(BACK TO THE BASICS OF LOVE)

Words and Music by BOBBY EMMONS
and CHIPS MOMAN

The on-ly two things in life that make it worth liv-in' is gui-tars that tune good and firm feel-in' wo-men. I don't need my name in the mar-quee lights; I got my song and I got you with me to-night. May-be it's time we got

Copyright © 1977 Songs Of PolyGram International, Inc. and Sony/ATV Songs LLC
All Rights Administered by Songs Of PolyGram International, Inc.
International Copyright Secured   All Rights Reserved

back to the basics of love. Let's go to Luck-en-bach, Tex - as, with Way-lon and Wil - lie and the boys. This suc-ces-ful life we're liv-in' got us feud-in' like the Hat-fields and Mc-Coys. Be-tween Hank Wil-liam's pain songs and New-ber-ry's train songs and

"Blue Eyes Cry-in' in the Rain," out in Luck-en-bach, Tex-as, ain't no-bod-y feel-in' no pain.

So, ba-by, let's sell your dia-mond ring, buy some boots and fad-ed jeans and go a-way. This coat and tie is cho-kin' me;____ In your high so-ci-e-ty you cry____ all day.

We've been so bus-y keep-in' up with the Jones'____ four car ga-rage, and we're still build-in' on, may-be it's time____ we got

D.S. and Fade

back to the ba-sics of love. Let's go to

NO ONE ELSE ON EARTH

Words and Music by SAM LORBER,
STEWART HARRIS and JILL COLUCCI

I've been a rock and I've got my fenc-es, I nev-er let them down.
You can make me want you an-y-time you want to, you're burn-in' me a-live.

Copyright © 1989 Sony/ATV Tunes LLC, Chalk Hill Music, Sony/ATV Songs LLC, Edisto Sound International, EMI Golden Torch Music Corp. and Heart Street Music
All Rights on behalf of Sony/ATV Tunes LLC, Chalk Hill Music, Sony/ATV Songs LLC and Edisto Sound International
Administered by Sony/ATV Music Publishing, 8 Music Square West, Nashville, TN 37203
All Rights on behalf of Heart Street Music Controlled and Administered by EMI Golden Torch Music Corp.
International Copyright Secured   All Rights Reserved

F
C
G
C
When it comes to love I
I can't de - ny you
F
C
G
C
keep my sens - es, I don't get kicked a - round.
e - ven when I catch you, weav - in' a weak al - i bi.
F
C
(1., D.S.) I shiv - ered once
Solo ends
'Cause when the night falls,
Fm/C
C
you broke in - to my soul. The dam-age is done now,
you make me for - get, your love is kill - ing me,

I'm out of con - trol.
and it ain't o - ver yet. How did you get to me?

No-one else on earth could ev - er hurt me, break my heart the way you do.

No-one else on earth was ev - er worth it.

No-one can love me like, no-one can love me like you.

you. *Guitar solo*

No-one else on earth could ev-er hurt me, break my heart the way you do. No-one else on earth was ev-er worth it. No-one can love me like, no-one can hurt me like,

Repeat and Fade

# OH, PRETTY WOMAN

Words and Music by ROY ORBISON
and BILL DEES

D
E7
wom - an
I don't be - lieve you, you're not the
wom - an
that you look love - ly as can
truth No - one could look as good as
be Are you lone - ly just like
no chord
you.
me?
Mer - cy.
1 E7
2 E7
Pret-ty

Pret-ty wom-an stop a - while, Pret-ty wom-an talk a - while, Pret-ty wom-an give your smile to me. Pret-ty wom-an yeah, yeah, yeah. Pret-ty wom-an

Am
Dm
look my way, Pret - ty wom - an
G7
C
A7
say you'll stay with me. "Cause I
F♯m
Dm
E7
need you I'll treat you right.
A
F♯m
Dm
Come with me ba - by. Be mine to -

night.

Pretty woman don't walk on by, Pretty woman don't make me cry Pretty woman don't walk a-way.

149

E7
Is she walk - ing back to
me?
Yeah, she's
walk - ing back to me!
A
Oh,
Pret - ty wom - an.

RING OF FIRE

Words and Music by MERLE KILGORE
and JUNE CARTER

Moderately Bright

Love _____ is a burn-ing thing _____
taste _____ of _____ love is sweet _____

And it makes _____ a fi-ry
When _____ hearts _____ like ours _____

Copyright © 1962, 1963 Painted Desert Music Corporation, New York
Copyright Renewed
International Copyright Secured   All Rights Reserved
Used by Permission

B♭ F7 B♭
ring
beat
B♭ E♭ B♭ E♭ B♭
Bound by wild de - sires
I fell for you like a child
F7 B♭
I fell in - to a Ring Of Fire.
Oh, but the fire went wild.
F7 E♭ B♭
I fell in - to a burn - ing Ring Of Fi - re I went

F7 Eb Bb F7
down, down, down and the flames went high - er And it
Bb F7 Bb
burns, burns, burns The Ring Of Fire
F7 1. Bb F7 2. Bb
The Ring Of Fire. The Fire.
F7 Bb F7
And it burns, burns, burns The Ring Of
Bb F7 Bb (Repeat for fadeout) F7
Fire, The Ring Of Fire. The Ring Of
dim.
dim.

PLEASE HELP ME, I'M FALLING
(IN LOVE WITH YOU)

Words and Music by DON ROBERTSON
and HAL BLAIR

Please help me, I'm fall - ing
oth - er
fall - ing

In love with you.
whose arms have grown cold.
and arms that would be sin.

Close the door to temp -
But I prom - ised for -
Close the door to temp -

ta - tion; don't let me walk through.
ev - er to have and to hold.
ta - tion; don't let me walk in.

Copyright © 1960 by Chappell & Co. and Don Robertson Music Corp.
Copyright Renewed
All Rights Administered by Chappell & Co.
International Copyright Secured   All Rights Reserved

Guitar tacet
F
F7
Turn a - way from me, dar - ling, I'm beg - ging you
So I can nev - er be free, dear, But when I'm with
For I must - n't want you, but, dar - ling, I
Bb
to. Please help me, I'm
you, I know that I'm
do. Please help me, I'm
F
C7
1,2 F
fall - ing in love with you.
los - ing the strength to be true.
fall - ing in love with
Guitar tacet
3 F
I be - long to an -
Please help me, I'm
you.

SNOWBIRD

Words and Music by
GENE MacLELLAN

Brightly

un - born grass lies wait - ing for its coat to turn to green.
thing that it would tell me that's the thing that I would do.
take the snow back with you where it came from on that day.
on - ly break my heart a - gain should I de - cide to stay.

The snow - bird sings the song he al - ways sings and
But now I feel such emp - ti - ness with - in for the
The one I love for - ev - er is un - true, and
So lit - tle snow - bird take me with you when you go to that

speaks to me of flow - ers that will bloom a - gain in
thing I want the most in life is the thing that I can't
if I could, you know that I would fly a - way with
land of gen - tle breez - es where the peace - ful wat - ers

1-3
C
spring.
win.
you.
When
The
4
C
flow.
G7
Yeah, if I could you know that I would
F
Dm7
fly a - way with
C
you.

WHEN YOU SAY NOTHING AT ALL

Words and Music by DON SCHLITZ
and PAUL OVERSTREET

Moderately slow

It's a-maz-ing how you can speak right to my heart.
All day long I can hear peo-ple talk-ing out loud,

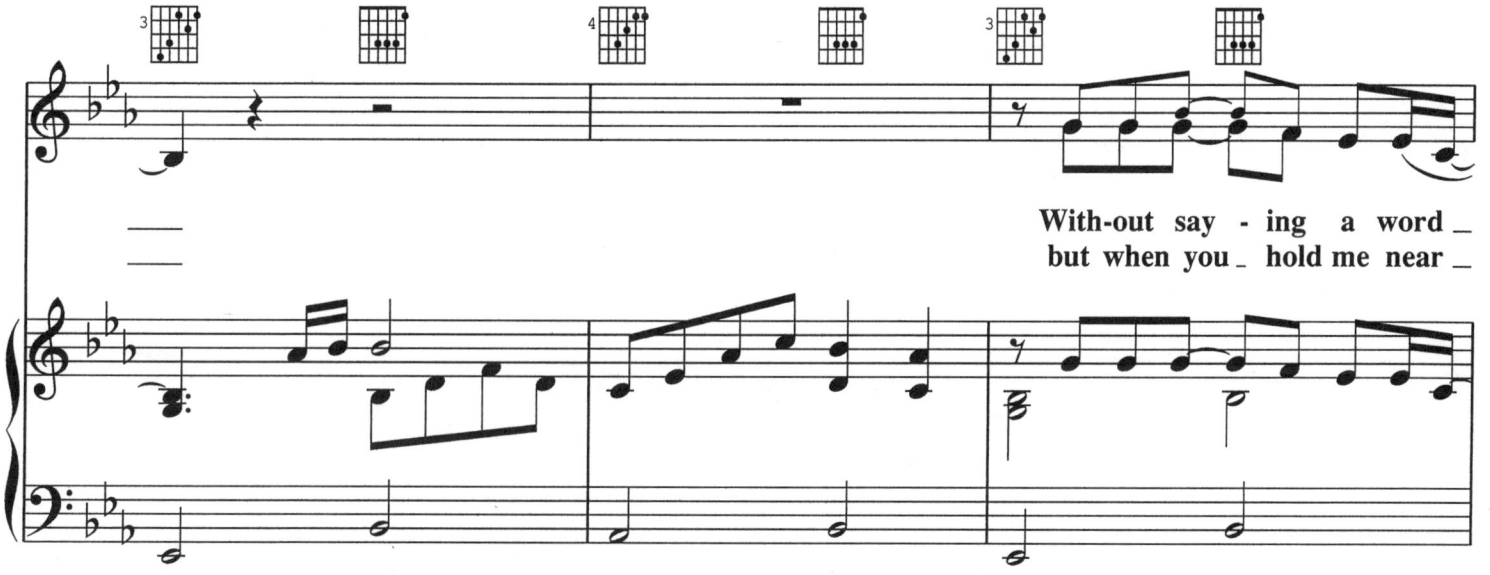

With-out say-ing a word
but when you hold me near

© Copyright 1988 by MCA MUSIC PUBLISHING, A Division of MCA INC., DON SCHLITZ MUSIC, SCREEN GEMS-EMI MUSIC INC. and SCARLET MOON MUSIC
All Rights for DON SCHLITZ MUSIC Controlled and Administered by MCA MUSIC PUBLISHING, A Division of MCA INC.
All Rights for SCARLET MOON MUSIC Administered by COPYRIGHT MANAGEMENT, INC., Nashville, TN
International Copyright Secured   All Rights Reserved

MCA music publishing

you can light up the dark.
you drown out the crowd.

Try as I may I could never explain
Old Mister Webster could never define

what I hear when you don't say a thing.
what's being said between your heart and mine.

The

smile on your face __ lets me know __ that you need __ me. There's a

truth in your eyes __ say-ing you'll __ nev-er leave __ me. A

touch of your hand _ says you'll catch _ me if ev - er I fall. __

Now you say it best __ when you say noth-ing at all. __

when you say noth-ing at all. __

when you say noth-ing at all.

WHEN YOU'RE HOT, YOU'RE HOT

Words and Music by
JERRY REED HUBBARD

Bright Tempo

(Spoken) (1) Well now,

me and Homer Jones and Big John Talley had a big crap game goin' back in the alley; and
time I rolled 'em dice I'd win, and I would just get ready to roll 'em a-gain, when I
took us into court I couldn't be-lieve my eyes__ The judge was a fishin' buddy that I recognised. I said, "Hey

I kept rollin' them sevens and winnin' all them pots. My
heard something behind me and I turned around and there was a big ole cop. He said,
Judge, old buddy old pal. I'll pay you that hundred I owe you if you get me out of this spot." So he

Copyright © 1971 Sixteen Stars Music and Vector Music
International Copyright Secured All Rights Reserved

Bb Eb Bb G7
luck was so good I could do no wrong. I just kept on rollin' and con - trollin' them bones.
"Hello Boy" and he gave us a grin, said, "Looks like I'm gonna have to haul you all in and keep
gave my friend a little fine to pay he turned around and grinned at me, and said,
C7 F7 Bb
fin-'ly they just threw up their hands and said, "When you're hot, you're hot." I said, "Yeah!
all that money for ev - i - dence." I said, "Well Son, When you're hot You're hot"
"Nine - ty days, Jerry, When you're hot, you're hot." I said, "Thanks a lot!"
Bb G7 C7 F7 Bb
(Sing) When you're hot, you're hot; And when you're not, you're not"
(Spoken) Put
(Spoken) You can
(Spoken) You let my
Bb G7 C7 F7 Bb
all the money in and let's roll 'em a-gain.
'splain if all down at city hall. (Sing) "When you're hot you're hot."
friends go free and throw the book at me. He said, "Well.

La la la la la la_____ la la la la la

la la la la la_____ When you're hot you're hot. *(Spoken)* Well, now ev-'ry
(Spoken) Well! When he

When you're hot you're hot. *(Spoken)* I said "Well I'll tell you, one thing judge, old
pick you up by the
Do you hear me?

Repeat and Fade

buddy, old pal. if you wasn't wearin' that black robe, I'd
court-house and I'd try a little bit of you on my own. You understand that!
Whose gonna collect my welfare? take over my Cadillac?

WHY NOT ME

Words and Music by HARLAN HOWARD,
SONNY THROCKMORTON and BRENT MAHER

Medium Country

You've been looking for love all around the world; baby,
searching from here to Singapore. Ain't it

don't you know this country girl's still free.
time that you noticed the girl next door. Baby,

Why not me?
Why not me?

Though you've fin-'ly come down to your
You had to see if the

Copyright © 1984 Sony/ATV Songs LLC, Sony/ATV Tunes LLC, Welbeck Music Corp. and Blue Quill Music
All Rights on behalf of Sony/ATV Songs LLC and Sony/ATV Tunes LLC Administered by Sony/ATV Music Publishing, 8 Music Square West, Nashville, TN 37203
All Rights on behalf of Welbeck Music Corp. and Blue Quill Music Controlled and Administered by EMI April Music Inc. under license from Sony/ATV Tunes LLC
International Copyright Secured   All Rights Reserved

old home town your Kentucky girl's been a-waiting patiently.
world was round. It's time that you learned how good settling down could be.

Why not me? Why not me on a rainy day? Why not me to love your cares away? Why not me? Why not me when the nights get cold?

D7
C
G
Why not me when you're grow - ing old?
Why not me?
1
2
D.S. al Coda (verse 1)
You've been
You've been
CODA
C
G
Why not me?
Why not me?
Dsus
G
Ba-by, why not me?

WOLVERTON MOUNTAIN

Words and Music by MERLE KILGORE
and CLAUDE KING

Moderately

1. They say don't
2. All of my
3. I'm go-ing

go _____ on Wol-ver-ton Mount-ain _____ If you're
dreams _____ are on Wol-ver-ton Mount-ain _____ I want his
up _____ on Wol-ver-ton Mount-ain _____ It's too

look-ing _____ for a wife _____ 'Cause Clif-ton
daugh-ter _____ for my wife _____ I'll take my
lone-some _____ down here be-low _____ It's just not

Clow-ers _____ has a pret-ty young daugh-ter _____ He's might-y
chanc-es _____ and climb that mount-ain _____ Though Clif-ton
right _____ to hide his daugh-ter _____ From the

Copyright © 1962 Painted Desert Music Corporation, New York
Copyright Renewed
International Copyright Secured   All Rights Reserved
Used by Permission

han - dy _____ with a gun _ and a knife: _____
Clow - ers _____ he may take _ my _ life: _____
one _____ who loves _ her _ so: _____

Chorus

Her ten - der lips _____ are sweet - er than hon - ey _____

And Wol - ver - ton Mount - ain _____ pro - tects her there _____

The bears _ and birds _____ tell Clif - ton Clow - ers _____

If a strang - er _____ should wan - der there _____ 2. All of my
3. I'm go - ing

3.
F Bb F C7
there. But I don't care a - bout Clif - ton
mf
F Bb F
Clow - ers I'm gon - na climb up on his mount - ain I'm gon - na
C7 F Bb F
take the girl I love I don't care a - bout Clif - ton Clow - ers I'm a gon - na
C7 F Bb F
climb up on that mount - ain And I'll get the one I love I don't
C7 F Bb F
care a - bout Clif - ton Clow - ers I'm gon - na find the one I love I don't
dim.
Repeat (ad lib) and fade out

WINGS OF A DOVE

Words and Music by
BOB FERGUSON

Moderately Bright

Verse

When trou-bles sur-round us, when e-vils come, The bod-y grows

No-ah had drift-ed on the flood man-y days, He searched for

Copyright © 1959 by Husky Music, Inc. and Larrick Music
Copyright Renewed
All Rights for the U.S. and Canada Administered by Unichappell Music Inc.
International Copyright Secured   All Rights Reserved

weak; the spirit grows numb.
land in various ways.

When these things beset us,
Troubles he had some

He doesn't forget us. He sends down His
but wasn't forgotten. He sent him His

love On the wings of a dove.
love On the wings of a dove.

3. When Jesus went down to the waters that day,
   He was baptized in the usual way.
   When it was done, God blessed His Son.
   He sent him His love On the wings of a dove.

Contemporary & Classic Country

More great country hits from Hal Leonard arranged for piano and voice with guitar chords.

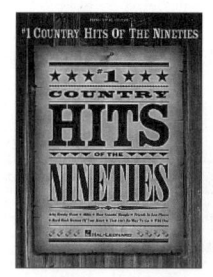

#1 Country Hits Of The Nineties
24 hot favorites, including: Achy Breaky Heart • Alibis • Boot Scootin' Boogie • Friends In Low Places • Hard Rock Bottom Of Your Heart • That Ain't No Way To Go • Wild One • and more.
00311699.................$10.95

Hot Country Dancin'
Over 30 toe-tapping, boot-scootin' favorites guaranteed to get you dancing! Includes: Achy Breaky Heart • Friends In Low Places • Here's A Quarter (Call Someone Who Cares) • Hey, Good Lookin' • I Feel Lucky • and more.
00311621.................$12.95

Country Inspiration
21 sentimental favorites, including: Brotherly Love • Guardian Angels • I Saw The Light • Love Can Build A Bridge • Love Without End, Amen • The Vows Go Unbroken • Why Me Lord? • and more.
00311616...................$9.95

51 Country Standards
A collection of 51 of country's biggest hits, including: (Hey Won't You Play) Another Somebody Done Somebody Wrong Song • By The Time I Get To Phoenix • Could I Have This Dance • Daddy Sang Bass • Forever And Ever, Amen • God Bless The U.S.A. • Green Grass Of Home • Islands In The Stream • King Of The Road • Little Green Apples • Lucille • Mammas Don't Let Your Babies Grow Up To Be Cowboys • Ruby Don't Take Your Love To Town • Stand By Me • Through The Years • Your Cheatin' Heart.
00359517.........................$14.95

The Award-Winning Songs Of The Country Music Association
Second Edition – Updated!
An update to the first edition, this songbook features 35 songs nominated for "Song of the Year" by the Country Music Association from 1984 through 1991. Songs include: Islands In The Stream • Chiseled In Stone • Don't Rock The Jukebox • Friends In Low Places • God Bless The U.S.A. • Grandpa (Tell Me 'Bout The Good Old Days) • On The Other Hand • All My Ex's Live In Texas • Forever And Ever, Amen.
00312476...$16.95

The Branson Songbook
As one of the most popular vacation destinations in the U.S. and more live music per mile than even Nashville, Branson, Missouri, has now become the new music mecca for more than 5 million tourists annually. This book celebrates the music and artists of this hot new spot with 19 songs, including: Moon River • Blue Velvet • Gentle On My Mind • Bubbles In The Wine • Yesterday When I Was Young • and many more. Also includes an introduction with photos.
00311693...$12.95

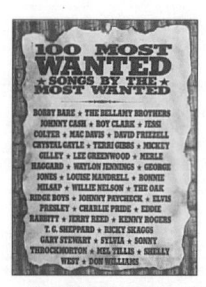

100 Most Wanted
Highlights: A Boy Named Sue • Break It To Me Gently • Crying My Heart Out Over You • Heartbroke • I.O.U. • I Know A Heartache When I See One • Mammas Don't Let Your Babies Grow Up To Be Cowboys • My Heroes Have Always Been Cowboys • Stand By Me • Save The Last Dance For Me • You're The First Time I've Thought About Leaving • You're The Reason God Made Oklahoma • many more.
00360730.........................$15.95

Cheatin' And Drinkin' Songs
47 country crooning classics, including: Daytime Friends • Don't The Girls All Get Prettier At Closin' Time • Friends In Low Places • I'm Gonna Hire A Wino To Decorate Our Home • Papa Loved Mama • Ruby Don't Take Your Love To Town • Straight Tequila Night • The Whiskey Ain't Workin' • Your Cheatin' Heart • and more.
00311618.........................$14.95

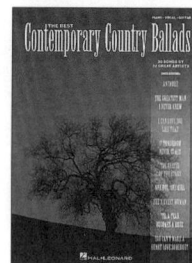

The Best Contemporary Country Ballads
30 heart-felt hits, including: After All This Time • The Greatest Man I Never Knew • I Can Love You Like That • I Meant Every Word He Said • One Boy, One Girl • When You Say Nothing At All • Where've You Been • more.
00310116.........................$14.95

90's Country Gold
29 chartburners, including: Achy Breaky Heart • Boot Scootin' Boogie • Down At The Twist And Shout • Friends In Low Places • I Feel Lucky • Neon Moon • Shameless • She Is His Only Need • Straight Tequila Night • and more.
00311607.........................$12.95

Country Love Songs – Updated
33 songs featuring: The Dance • For The Good Times • I Never Knew Love • Love Can Build A Bridge • She Is His Only Need • The Vows Go Unbroken (Always True To You) • and more.
00311528.........................$12.95

Great Ladies Of Country Music
Features 31 songs by 28 top female performers, such as: Mary Chapin Carpenter, Rosanne Cash, Patsy Cline, Emmylou Harris, Faith Hill, Kathy Mattea, Reba McEntire, Dolly Parton, Pam Tillis, and others. Songs include: I Fall To Pieces • Mi Vida Loca • Shut Up And Kiss Me • XXX's and OOO's • and more.
00310118.........................$14.95

FOR MORE INFORMATION, SEE YOUR LOCAL MUSIC DEALER, OR WRITE TO:

HAL•LEONARD CORPORATION
7777 W. BLUEMOUND RD. P.O. BOX 13819 MILWAUKEE, WI 53213

Prices, contents, and availability subject to change without notice.

0496